The Street Lawyer

John Grisham

Level 4

Retold by Michael Dean

Series Editors: Andy Hopkins and Jocelyn Potter

Pearson Education Limited
Edinburgh Gate, Harlow,
Essex CM20 2JE, England
and Associated Companies throughout the world.

Pack ISBN: 978-1-4058-5223-4
Book ISBN: 978-1-4058-5090-2
CD-ROM ISBN: 978-1-4058-5089-6

First published in Great Britain by Century, one of the publishers in
The Random House Group Limited 1998
First edition published by Penguin Books 2001
This edition published 2007

3 5 7 9 10 8 6 4 2

Original © Belfrey Holdings, Inc. 1998
Text copyright © Penguin Books Ltd 2001
This edition copyright © Pearson Education Ltd 2007
Illustrations by Carlos Puerta

Set in 11/13pt A. Garamond
Printed in China
SWTC/02
Produced for the Publishers by AC Estudio Editorial S.L.

Published by Pearson Education Ltd in association with Penguin Books Ltd,
both companies being subsidiaries of Pearson Plc

Acknowledgements
We are grateful to the following for permission to reproduce photographs:
Page 74: (top left) © Gary I. Rothstein/epa/Corbis; (middle top) © Alamy Royalty-Free;
(top right) © Alison Wright/CORBIS; (bottom left) © Gary Braasch/CORBIS;
(bottom right) © John Maier/Still Pictures
Every effort has been made to trace the copyright holders and we apologise in advance for any
unintentional omissions. We would be pleased to insert the appropriate
acknowledgement in any subsequent edition of this publication.

For a complete list of the titles available in the Penguin Active Reading series please write to your local
Pearson Longman office or to: Penguin Readers Marketing Department, Pearson Education,
Edinburgh Gate, Harlow, Essex CM20 2JE, England.

Contents

1.1 What's the book about?

1 **Read the information on the back cover of the book.**

The hero of this book, Michael, is a young lawyer. Which of these professionals is most useful to other people, in your opinion? Think of their value to other people's lives and put them in order.

> a doctor   a teacher   a lawyer   a policeman

2 **Lawyers are some of the most unpopular professionals in the United States. Why is that? Look on the Internet for "lawyer jokes." List four things that people dislike about them.**

a ....

b ....

c ....

d ....

1.2 What happens first?

1 **Look at this photo. Discuss whether the professionals in 1.1 above live and/or work in this kind of area. Why (not)?**

2 **The hero of this book is a successful lawyer. At the beginning of the book, do you think Michael is:**

a   a rich man?   **Yes / No**

b   a happy man?   **Yes / No**

c   a good man?   **Yes / No**

PENGUIN ACTIVE READING   *LEVEL 4*

The Street Lawyer
John Grisham

CHAPTER 1

Mister

Mister pointed at the dynamite around his waist.
"I pull this," he said, "and we die."

The old black man got into the elevator behind me. He smelled of smoke and cheap wine and life on the streets without soap. His beard and hair were half-gray and very dirty. He was wearing sunglasses, and a long dirty coat hung down to his knees.

He looked fat, probably because he had all his clothes on. In the winter in Washington the street people wear all their clothes all the time. They can't leave any of their clothes at home, because they don't have a home.

The old man didn't belong here. Everything here was expensive. The 400 lawyers in the building, who all worked for Drake & Sweeney, were paid an unbelievable amount of money. I knew that because I was a Drake & Sweeney lawyer myself.

The elevator stopped at six. The man hadn't pushed an elevator button. When I stepped out and turned right, he followed me. I pushed the heavy, wooden door of a big meeting room. There were eight lawyers at the table inside and they all looked surprised. They were looking behind me, so I turned. My friend from the elevator was standing there. He was pointing a gun at me.

"Put that gun down," said one of the lawyers at the table. His name was Rafter. He was a hard man in a courtroom, maybe the hardest lawyer that Drake & Sweeney had.

Suddenly, a shot hit the ceiling. Rafter's eyes opened wide and his mouth shut.

"Lock the door," the man said to me. I locked the door of the meeting room.

"Stand against the wall." We all stood against the wall.

The man took off his dirty coat and put it carefully on the large, expensive table in the center of the room. He had five or six red sticks around his waist, tied there with string. I had never seen **dynamite** before, but they looked like dynamite to me.

I wanted to run and hope for a bad shot when he fired at me. But my legs were like water. Some of the lawyers were shaking with fear and making noises like scared animals.

"Please be quiet," said the man, calmly. Then he took a long yellow rope and a knife from the pocket of his pants. "You," he said to me. "Tie them up."

Rafter stepped forward. "Listen, friend," he said, "what do you want?"

The second shot went into the wall, behind Rafter's ear.

"Do not call me 'friend,'" said the man.

"What would you like us to call you?" I asked him, quietly.

"Call me 'Mister.'"

I tied the eight lawyers with the yellow rope. One of them, Barry Nuzzo, was my friend. We were the same age, thirty-two, and we had started at Drake & Sweeney on the same day. Only our marriages were different. His was successful and mine wasn't. He had three kids. Claire and I didn't have any. I looked at Barry and he looked at me. I knew we were both thinking about Barry's kids.

We could hear police cars outside and noises as the police entered the building. Mister pointed at the dynamite around his waist.

"I pull this," he said, "and we die."

For a second we all looked at each other, nine white boys and "Mister."

I thought of all those terrible shootings you read about in the newspapers. A crazy worker returns to work after lunch with a gun and kills everybody in his office. There had been killings at fast-food restaurants and playgrounds, too. And those dead people were children or honest workers. Who would care about us? We were lawyers.

Time passed.

"What did you eat for lunch today?" Mister asked me, breaking a long silence.

dynamite /ˈdaɪnəmaɪt/ (n) something that causes a powerful explosion

He spoke clearly and, from the sound of his voice, he had had a good education. He hadn't always been on the streets.

"I had chicken and salad," I said, surprised.

"Alone?"

"No, I met a friend."

"How much did it cost, for both of you?"

"Thirty dollars."

Mister didn't like that. "Thirty dollars," he repeated. "For two people. You know what I had for lunch?"

"No."

"I had soup. Free soup from a **shelter** and I was glad to get it. You could feed a hundred of my friends for thirty dollars, you know that?"

"Yes, Mister."

"Call your boss."

There was a phone on the table. I called Arthur Jacobs. Eight hundred lawyers worked for Drake & Sweeney around the world, but at seventy-nine Jacobs was the oldest of the partners here in Washington. He answered at the first ring of the phone.

"Mr. Jacobs?"

"Michael! Are you OK?"

"Wonderful," I said.

"What does he want from us?"

I spoke to the man: "What do you want, Mister?"

"Soup with bread," said the man. "Get it from the shelter at L Street and 17th. They put a lot of vegetables in the soup there."

"One soup with bread," I said into the phone.

"No," said the man. "Get soup and bread for all of us."

"Mr. Jacobs . . . " I said.

"I heard. I can hear him. A shelter for street people does carryouts?"

"Mr. Jacobs. Please just do it. He has a gun and dynamite."

I put the phone down.

"You," said the man. He was talking to me. "What's your name?"

"Michael Brock."

"How much money did you earn last year? Don't lie."

I thought quickly. I didn't lie. "A hundred and twenty thousand."

He didn't like that. "How much did you give to poor people?"

"I don't remember. My wife does that."

"Thank you, Mr. Brock."

shelter /ˈʃɛltə/ (n) a place that protects you from danger or the weather

Mister pointed the gun at the other lawyers. He asked all of them the same questions. Nate Malamud, the only partner in the room, earned more than a million dollars.

"More than a million?" Mister said to him. "I know you. You walk past me when I sit on the sidewalk every morning. You never give me any money. Why can't you help poor people, homeless people?"

Nate was a big man with white hair. He had been with Drake & Sweeney for thirty years. He was red in the face with embarrassment now. "I'm sorry," he said.

"Who did the **evict**ion?" said Mister, suddenly. And again, "Who did the eviction?"

Nobody spoke. None of us understood him. But Mister wasn't looking for an answer. He looked out the window. Maybe he was thinking. Maybe he was dreaming. Maybe he was watching the police out there.

Our soup and bread arrived half an hour later. There was a knock on the door and somebody outside shouted through the door, "Your food."

Mister shouted back: "If I see a policeman out there, I'll kill these men."

Then he pointed the gun at my head. The two of us walked slowly to the door. "Unlock the door and open it very slowly," Mister said.

There was nobody outside. The food was on the floor, near the door.

As I stepped outside and bent down to pick it up, I heard a shout: "Stay down!" A policeman stepped quickly out of the office opposite and shot Mister through the head.

Mister fell without a sound, and my face was covered in blood. Whose blood? Mister was lying on the floor. Half his head had gone, but the sunglasses still covered one eye. His hands were nowhere near the dynamite.

Policemen came running from all the offices. "Are you hurt?" one of them asked me.

I didn't know. I couldn't see. There was blood on my face and shirt and a liquid that, I discovered later, was part of Mister's brain.

evict /ɪ'vɪkt/ (v) to legally force someone to leave their home

CHAPTER 2

DeVon Hardy

*"Who did the eviction?" Mister had asked. But I guess
he already knew the answer to that.*

A policeman led me to the first floor of the building, where friends and family
and doctors were waiting. The doctors crowded around, but where was my
wife? Six hours in a room with a gunman, and she hadn't come to see me. It was
funny really because my wife, Claire, was a doctor herself, at one of the biggest
hospitals in Washington.

I lay on a table for ten minutes while doctors examined me to make sure I was
all right. Then my secretary, Polly, arrived. There were tears in her eyes as she
put her arms around me.

"Where's Claire?" I asked her.

"I called the hospital. She's working."

Polly knew there wasn't much left of the marriage.

"Are you OK?" she asked.

"I think so."

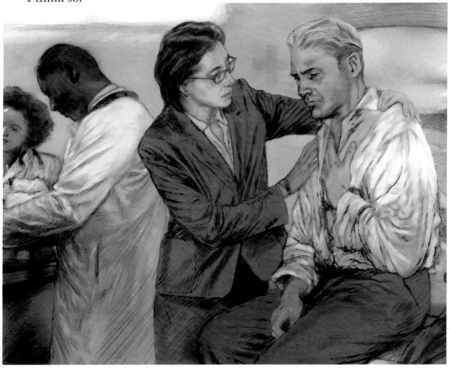

"I'll take you home."

I was pleased someone was telling me what to do. My thoughts came into my head slowly. It was like I was under water.

We left the Drake & Sweeney building by a back door. There were police cars everywhere and ambulances and television vans, even a fire truck.

"I'm alive! I'm alive!" I realized, smiling for the first time. "I'm alive." I looked up to heaven and said a very big "thank you." When I got home to our apartment on P Street in Georgetown, Claire wasn't there.

I sat in the empty apartment and thought about her. We had met the week after I moved to Washington. I was just out of Yale with a great job. She came from one of America's oldest families. We were in love, we got married.

But Drake & Sweeney make you work very hard the first year. I worked fifteen hours a day, six days a week. I saw Claire on Sundays and we went out together when I wasn't too tired.

For the last five years I had worked about 200 hours a month. That's eight hours every day for six days with two or three hours on Sunday.

But young lawyers at Drake & Sweeney don't complain about long hours. Fewer than one in ten become partners, and everybody wants to be that one in ten because you earn at least a million dollars a year.

Claire was good about it for the first few months, but then she got tired of having a husband who was never there and I didn't blame her. There are a lot of **divorce**s at Drake & Sweeney. Long hours at work, each hour paid for by a **client**, are more important than a happy wife.

By the end of our first year together, Claire was unhappy and we weren't talking together very much. She decided to go to medical school and I thought that was a great idea. Drake & Sweeney were telling me that I was a possible future partner. I just had to work even harder. When Claire was studying, I didn't feel so guilty about that.

But Claire didn't just study. She worked unbelievably long hours. She had decided she wanted to be a great doctor. Soon we were playing a crazy game called "I-can-work-harder-than-you." And another game called "my job is more important than your job because I'm a doctor/lawyer."

My boss, Arthur Jacobs, of course, was on my team. He had become a partner in Drake & Sweeney at the age of thirty. The youngest ever partner. And he would soon be the oldest ever working partner. The law was his life. All three of his divorced wives could tell you that.

---

divorce /dəˈvɔrs/ (n/v) the legal ending of a marriage
client /ˈklaɪənt/ (n) someone who pays for advice or services from a person or organization

I woke up suddenly. I had fallen asleep in an armchair at the apartment and Claire was sitting in a chair next to me.

"Where were you today?" I said.

"At the hospital."

"At the hospital? Nine of us are in a room with a crazy man and a gun for six hours. We get lucky and escape. Eight families come and see their relative because they're interested in whether or not he's alive. And how do I get home? My secretary drives me."

"I couldn't be there."

"Oh, no! Of course you couldn't be there. How silly of me!"

"I couldn't be there because the police asked all doctors to stay at their hospitals until the situation at Drake & Sweeney ended. They always do that when there's a possible shooting."

"Oh. Did you call?"

"I tried. I guess there were a lot of people trying."

◆

Next morning we made breakfast together. We ate in the kitchen, watching the small television. The six o'clock news showed the Drake & Sweeney building, and you could see Mister looking out of the window.

The television news said the dynamite wasn't real. The sticks were made of wood and Mister had painted them red. The gun was real enough, though. It was a .44, stolen. Mister's real name was DeVon Hardy. He was forty-five. He had fought in Vietnam. He had been in prison a few times for stealing, but he wasn't a big criminal. And he was homeless with no known family.

That morning's *Washington Post* had more details.

According to someone called Mordecai Green, the **Director** of the 14th Street Law Center, DeVon Hardy had recently lost his job. Then he became homeless.

He was living in an old **warehouse**. This wasn't unusual. A lot of homeless people move into empty buildings because they have no money for their own place.

DeVon Hardy had recently been evicted from the warehouse, as an illegal **squatter**. Lawyers are responsible for evictions. "Who did the eviction?" Mister had asked. But I guess he already knew the answer to that.

And now I knew it, too. Drake & Sweeney had thrown Mister into the streets.

---

director /dɪ'rektər, daɪ-/ (n) someone who controls or manages a company or organization
warehouse /'wɛrhaʊs/ (n) a big building for storing large quantities of things
squatter /'skwɑtə/ (n) someone who lives in a building without permission and without paying rent

Activities 2

2.1 Were you right?

Look at your answers to Activity 1.2.2 on page iv.

1 How much money did Michael earn last year? ....

2 Why is Michael unhappy? ....

....

3 In your opinion, how could Michael be a better person? ....

....

....

....

....

....

2.2 What more did you learn?

What more did you learn? Answer these questions. Write the names.

1 Who may be Drake & Sweeney's hardest lawyer?

....

2 Who is thirty-two years old and has three children?

....

3 Who has been at Drake & Sweeney for almost fifty years?

....

4 Who earned more than a million dollars last year?

....

5 Who has no children and works as a doctor in a Washington hospital?

....

6 Who is the Director of the 14th Street Law Center?

....

7 Who recently lost his job and was evicted from his home?

....

2.3 Language in use

Look at the sentence on the right. Then put the information in the sentences below into a single sentence in the same way. Use *who, which* or *whose*.

> The 400 lawyers in the building, **who all worked for Drake & Sweeney,** were paid an unbelievable amount of money.

1 DeVon Hardy was wearing all his clothes. The clothes were very dirty.
DeVon Hardy was wearing all his clothes, which were very dirty.

2 The lawyers looked surprised. The lawyers weren't expecting visitors.

3 Mister tied the lawyers up. Mister's real name was DeVon Hardy.

4 Mr. Jacobs spoke to the L Street shelter. The shelter gave free soup to the poor.

5 Mister wanted to know who was responsible for the eviction. Mister was homeless.

6 Drake & Sweeney lawyers didn't complain about long hours. The lawyers worked fifteen hours a day.

2.4 What's next?

Discuss this question and circle your answer.

1 Michael believes that Drake & Sweeney evicted DeVon Hardy from his home. If the eviction was illegal, Drake & Sweeney have committed a crime. They may be responsible for the old man's death. What do you think Michael will do?

a Nothing. It's not his business.

b Find out about the eviction, but keep quiet about it, because Drake & Sweeney are his employers.

c Find out about the eviction and go to the police or the newspapers.

CHAPTER 3

Mordecai Green

*Mordecai Green was a warm, caring man whose work was
on the streets. He was a lawyer with a heart.*

I had told Polly I would be at work today—the day after Mister came into the
office. But for the first time ever, I didn't go to work when I was well enough
to go. Just as it started to snow, I got into my car, a Lexus, and drove through the
streets of Washington. The snow came down harder and harder. I just drove.

Polly's voice came over the car phone. She sounded worried. "Where are you?"

"Who wants to know?"

"A lot of people. Arthur Jacobs wants to see you. You have clients waiting for
you."

"I'm fine, Polly. Tell everybody I'm at the doctor's office."

"Are you?"

"No, but I could be."

I drove around Georgetown, not going anywhere, just driving. The clouds were dark. The snow would be heavy. People were hurrying through the snow on the sidewalks. I saw a homeless man and wondered if he knew DeVon Hardy. Where do street people go in a snowstorm?

I called the hospital. I wanted to ask Claire to meet me for lunch. But the hospital said Claire was busy and they couldn't contact her. That was the end of our lunch together.

I turned and went northeast, past Logan Circle, into the gang area of the city, and drove until I found the 14th Street Law Center. I parked at 14th and Q, certain that I would never see the expensive Lexus again.

The 14th Street Law Center was in an old, tall, red brick house that had seen better days. The windows on the top floor were protected by pieces of wood over the glass. The door wasn't locked. I went in slowly, out of the snow, and entered another world.

It was a law office all right, but there was no expensive furniture here, not like at Drake & Sweeney. I stepped into a large room which had three metal desks, each covered in **files**. There were more files on old pieces of carpet on the floor. The computers and the only **photocopier** were ten years old. There was a large photograph of Martin Luther King on one wall. The office was busy and dusty and interesting.

"You looking for somebody?" asked a woman at a desk with the name Sofia Mendoza on it. She looked Mexican. She wasn't smiling, but I did. It was funny. Nobody at Drake & Sweeney would talk to a visitor like that. They would lose their job. But I would soon learn how important Sofia was to the 14th Street Law Center.

"I'm looking for Mordecai Green," I said. But just then he came out of his office. Sofia went back to her work.

Green was an enormous black man, at least two meters tall and very heavy. He was in his early fifties, with a gray beard and round red glasses. He shouted something about a file to Sofia and then turned to me.

"Can I help you?"

"I want to talk to you about DeVon Hardy," I said and gave him my Drake & Sweeney card.

---

file /faɪl/ (n) a collection of papers containing information about a person or subject

photocopier /ˈfəʊtəˌkɒpiə/ (n) a machine that copies documents onto paper

He looked at me for a few seconds and then looked quickly at Sofia, who was speaking in fast Spanish into the phone. Mordecai Green walked back into his office and I followed him in. The office was a small room with no windows and the desk and floor covered in files and law books.

"Sit down," he said. "But you might get dirty. What do you want?"

I sat down. "I was in the room with DeVon Hardy when he was shot," I said. "I couldn't think this morning. I didn't want to go to work. So I came here. Any idea why he did it?"

"Because of the eviction," said Mordecai Green. "A few months ago he moved into an old warehouse at the corner of Florida **Avenue**. It wasn't a bad place for a homeless person. It had a roof, some toilets, water."

"Who owned the warehouse?"

Mordecai pulled a thin file from one of the piles on his desk. It was exactly the one he wanted. He looked at the file for a minute.

"The warehouse was owned by a company called RiverOaks."

"And RiverOaks's lawyers are Drake & Sweeney?"

"Probably."

"Is that all?"

"No. I heard that DeVon Hardy and the others got no warning of the eviction."

"But you can evict squatters with no warning."

"Oh yes. You can't evict **tenant**s without a warning, though."

"Was DeVon Hardy a squatter or a tenant?"

"I don't know."

I thought of another question. "How did DeVon Hardy know about Drake & Sweeney?"

"Who knows? He wasn't stupid, though. Crazy, but not stupid."

I had taken enough of his time. He looked at his watch, I looked at mine. We exchanged phone numbers and promised to stay in contact.

Mordecai Green was a warm, caring man whose work was on the streets, protecting hundreds of nameless clients. He was a lawyer with a heart.

On the way out, Sofia didn't look up from her conversation on the phone. The Lexus was still there, covered by an inch of snow.

avenue /ˈævəˌnu/ (n) a big street in a town or city
tenant /ˈtɛnənt/ (n) someone who lives in a house or room and pays rent to the owner

14

CHAPTER 4

Mom and Dad

"Welcome to the world, son. You think the guys in factory jobs like what they're doing? You're getting rich, they aren't."

After I left Mordecai Green's office, I drove around and around the city while the snow fell. As a lawyer with hours to work, which my clients paid for, I couldn't do this sort of thing—just moving with the traffic, not going anywhere. But I was doing it now.

I didn't want to go back to the empty apartment. I didn't want to go to a bar, either—I'd probably never leave. So I drove. I went through poor parts of the city I had never seen before.

Then I went back to Drake & Sweeney. I went up in Mister's elevator again, walked along the hall to my office, and sat down at my desk. For the first time I wondered how much everything in my office had cost—the expensive old desk, the red leather armchairs, and the Persian carpets. Weren't we just chasing money, here in this building? Why did we work so hard to buy a more expensive carpet or an older desk? Was that a good reason to work? Was this the life I wanted?

In my expensive room, I thought of Mordecai Green, giving his time to help people who had nothing.

I had about ten pink telephone messages from clients on my desk and none of them interested me. I didn't like this work. My clients were big companies, and I worked on their **lawsuit**s against other big companies. The lawsuits continued for years. Maybe a hundred lawyers worked on each one, all sending paper to each other.

Polly came in and brought me cookies. She put them on the table with a big smile before she left for home for the day. A couple of lawyers came in, said "How you doin'?" and left again. They were probably on their way home too.

Alone in the office again, I picked up one big file and then another one. Which lawsuit did I want to work on today? I didn't want to work on any of them. I couldn't do it. It didn't make any sense to me now.

I went to my computer and began searching our client files. RiverOaks was started in 1977 in Hagerstown, Maryland. It was a private company, so it was difficult to get information about it.

RiverOaks was the client of a Drake & Sweeney lawyer called Braden Chance. I didn't know the name but I looked again in our computer files. Braden Chance

lawsuit /'lɔsut/ (n) a disagreement between two people or organizations that is taken to a court of law for a decision

was a partner in **real estate**, on the fourth floor. He was forty-four years old, married, and went to law school at Duke.

There were forty-two files for RiverOaks. Four were about evictions. RiverOaks had bought a warehouse on Florida Avenue. On January 27, some squatters were evicted from the warehouse—one of them, as I now knew, was DeVon Hardy. The file on the eviction itself had a number next to it. The number meant that only Braden Chance could open the file. I wrote down the file's name and number and walked down to the fourth floor.

When I got there, I saw a legal assistant and asked him where Braden Chance's office was. He pointed to an open door across the hall. Although it was late, Chance was at his desk, looking busy. He didn't like me just walking in from the hall. At Drake & Sweeney, you phoned first and made an appointment. But that didn't worry me very much.

real estate /ˈrɪəl ɪˌsteɪt/ (n) property like houses or land

Chance didn't ask me to sit down, but I did and he didn't like that either.

"You were next to the guy when he got shot," he said unpleasantly, after I said DeVon Hardy's name.

"Yes," I said.

"Terrible for you, huh?"

"It's over. Mr. Hardy, who's now dead, was evicted from a warehouse. Was it one of our evictions?"

"It was," said Chance, but he didn't look at me as he spoke. I guessed that Arthur Jacobs had looked at the file with him, earlier in the day. "What about it?" added Chance.

"Was he a squatter?"

"Of course he was. They're all squatters, aren't they? Our client just got them out of the warehouse."

"Are you sure he was a squatter? Not a tenant?"

Chance looked angry. "What do you want?"

"Could I see the file?"

"No."

"Why not?"

"I'm very busy. Will you please leave?"

"If he was a squatter, there's no problem. Why can't I see the file?"

"Because it's mine, and I said no. How's that?"

"Maybe that's not good enough."

He stood, his hands shaking as he pointed to the door. I smiled at him and left. The legal assistant from the hall had heard everything and we exchanged looks and smiles as I passed his desk. "The man's a fool," he said, very quietly. I smiled again. "Yes."

But what was Chance hiding? There was something wrong and it was in that file. I had to get it. I went back to my office to think. The phone rang. It was Claire.

"Why are you at the office?" She spoke very slowly and her voice was colder than the snow outside.

I looked at my watch. I remembered we had arranged to have dinner together at the apartment. "I, uh, well, a client called from the West Coast." I had used this lie before. It didn't matter.

"I'm waiting, Michael. Should I start to eat?"

"No, I'll be back at the apartment as fast as I can."

I ran from the building into the snowstorm, but I didn't really care that another evening together had been ruined.

◆

A few hours later, Claire and I were having our coffee by the kitchen window. The snow had finally stopped. I had an idea. "Let's go to Florida," I said.

She gave me a cold look. "Florida?"

"OK, the Bahamas. We can leave tomorrow."

"It's impossible."

"Not at all. I don't have to work for a few days . . . "

"Why not?"

"Because I'm going crazy, and at Drake & Sweeney if you go crazy, then you get a few days off."

"You *are* going crazy."

"I know. It's fun, actually. People are nice to you. They smile. Polly brought me cookies today. I like it."

The cold look returned and she said, "I can't."

And that was the end of that. I knew she couldn't do it. She was a doctor, people had appointments with her. But also, she didn't want to go with me.

"OK," I said. "Then I'm going to Memphis for a couple of days to see my parents."

"Oh really," she said. She didn't even sound interested.

"I need to see my parents. It's been almost a year. And this is a good time, I think. I don't like the snow and I don't feel like working. Like I said, I'm going crazy."

Claire got up and went to bed. "Well, call me," she said over her shoulder. I knew that was the end of my marriage. And I hated to have to tell my mother.

◆

My parents were in their early sixties and trying to enjoy not working for the first time in their lives. Mom had been a bank manager. Dad had been a lawyer in Atlanta. They had worked hard, saved hard, and given me the best of everything. Dad always wanted me to be a lawyer, like him.

I rented a car at Memphis airport and drove east to the rich part of the city where the white people live. The blacks had the center of the city and the whites the area outside. Sometimes the blacks moved out from the center into a white area and then the whites moved further out.

My parents lived on a **golf course** in a new glass house. You could see the golf course from every window. I had called from the airport, so Mom knew I was coming.

"What's wrong?" she asked when she saw me.

"Nothing. I'm fine."

golf course /'gɑlf kɔrs, 'gɔlf-/ (n) an area of land where you play golf

"Where's Claire? You guys never call us, you know. I haven't heard her voice in two months."

"Claire's fine, Mom. We're both alive and healthy and working very hard."

"Are you spending enough time together?"

"No."

"Are you spending any time together?"

"Not much." I saw the tears in her eyes. "I'm sorry, Mom. It's lucky we don't have kids."

To talk about something else, I told her the story of Mister.

"Are you all right?" she asked, a look of shock on her face.

"Of course. I'm here, aren't I? The company wanted me to take a couple of days' holiday, so I came home."

"You poor thing. Claire, and now this."

Later that afternoon, my dad and I played **golf**.

"Dad, I'm not very happy at Drake & Sweeney," I said. "I don't like what I'm doing."

"Welcome to the world, son. You think the guys in factory jobs like what they're doing? You're getting rich, they aren't. Be happy."

He was happy. He was winning at the golf. Ten minutes later he said, "Are you changing jobs?"

"I'm thinking about it."

"Why don't you just say what you're trying to say?"

As usual, I felt weak and like I was running away from something.

"I'm thinking about working for the homeless," I said. "As a lawyer," I added quickly.

Dad didn't stop playing. He hit a ball into the distance. "I'd hate to see you throw it all away, son," he said. "You'll be a partner in a few years." We walked after his ball. "A street guy's killed in front of you and you have to change the world? You just need a few days away from work."

Is that all?

---

golf /ˈɡɑːlf, ˈɡɒːlf/ (n) a game in which you hit a small white ball into holes in the ground

3.1 **Were you right?**

Look back at Activity 2.4. What does Michael decide to do about:

1 DeVon Hardy's death? ....

....

2 his marriage? ....

....

3 his job? ....

....

3.2 **What more did you learn?**

1 Compare the 14th Street Law Center with Michael's office at Drake & Sweeney. In which office or offices can these be found?

metal desks   Persian carpets   an old photocopier   windows
pieces of carpets   a computer   files   a photo of Martin Luther King
red leather armchairs   dust and dirt   an expensive desk

The Law Center	Michael's office	Both offices
metal desks		

2 Who says these words? Write the names. Then discuss what they tell you about that person and their part in the story.

a "You looking for somebody?" ....

b "Sit down. But you might get dirty." ....

c "Because it's mine, and I said no." ....

d "I'm waiting, Michael. Should I start to eat?" ....

e "Are you spending any time together?" ....

f "Welcome to the world, son." ....

.3 Language in use

Look at the sentence on the right. Then write similar sentences.

> **I haven't heard** her voice **in** two months.

1 Michael and Claire last had a vacation three years ago.
   They haven't had a vacation in three years.

2 It's almost a year since Michael saw his parents.
   ....
   ....

3 Michael last took a day off work over eighteen months ago.
   ....
   ....

4 Michael and Claire last went out for dinner together four months ago.
   ....
   ....

5 Michael's father and mother gave up work three years ago.
   ....
   ....

6 It is about two years since Michael beat his father at golf.
   ....
   ....

7 Michael's mother last saw Claire months ago.
   ....
   ....

3.4 What's next?

Michael is changing. He is moving toward being a "lawyer with a heart." What do you think? Write *Yes* or *No*.

1 Will he take his father's advice and go back to work? ....

2 Will he give up working for Drake & Sweeney completely? ....

3 Will he spend more time with his wife and maybe save his marriage? ....

CHAPTER 5

Lontae Burton

*Inside were a young mother and her children, all dead. The mother had
started the engine of the old car and left it running.*

O f course the apartment was empty when I returned Friday night, but
there was a note in the kitchen. Just like me, Claire had gone home to
her parents in Providence for a couple of days. I knew Claire wanted to end the
marriage, too. I just didn't know how badly.

I went for a long walk. It was very cold outside, with a strong wind. I passed
beautiful homes with families in them, eating and laughing and enjoying the
warmth.

Then I moved onto M Street. Friday night on M was always fun time; the
bars and coffee shops were full, and people were waiting in line to get into the
restaurants.

I stopped at the window of a music club, listening to sad music with snow over my feet, watching the young couples drink and dance. For the first time in my life, I didn't feel young. I was thirty-two, but in the last five years I had worked more than most people do in twenty. I was tired. Those pretty girls in there would never look at me now.

I went back to the apartment. At some time after nine, the phone rang. It was Mordecai Green. "Are you busy?" he asked.

"To do what?"

"To work. The shelters are full. We don't have enough helpers."

"I've ... never done that kind of work."

"Can you put butter on bread?"

"I think so."

"Then you're the man for us. We're at a church on 13th and Euclid."

"I'll be there in twenty minutes."

I changed into the oldest clothes I had, jeans and an old blue jacket, and took most of my money out of my wallet. As I closed the apartment door behind me, I was excited and I didn't exactly know why.

I parked the Lexus opposite the church. The attack I half expected didn't happen. No gangs. The snow kept the streets empty and safe, for now. I went into the church, down into a big room below it, and entered the world of the homeless.

It was unbelievable how many people were in that room. **Volunteer**s were giving out blankets and apples. Mordecai was pouring fruit juice into paper cups and talking all the time. A line waited patiently for food at a table.

I went to Mordecai and he said hello like I was an old friend. "It's crazy," he said. "One big snowstorm and we work all night." He showed me the bread, the butter, the meat, and the cheese. "It's real complicated. You do ten with meat and then ten with cheese. OK?"

"Yeah."

"You learn fast." Then he disappeared.

I made ten sandwiches quickly, then I slowed and watched all the people. Most of the homeless looked down at the floor. Most of them said "thank you" to the volunteers when they got the food. Then they ate slowly. Even the children were careful with their food.

Mordecai came back and started making sandwiches next to me. "Where does the food come from?" I asked him.

"Food bank. People give it. Tonight we're lucky because we have chicken— usually it's just vegetables."

volunteer /ˌvɑlən'tɪr/ (n) someone who offers to do something for no pay

"How many shelters like this are there in the city?"

"This isn't actually a shelter. The church kindly opens its doors when the weather's bad. When the doors close, they go out again."

I tried to understand this. "Then where do these people live?"

"Some are squatters. They're the lucky ones. Some live on the streets, some in parks, some in bus stations, some under bridges. Usually it's OK, but they can't stay out in the open tonight. It's too cold. They have to go to one of the shelters."

"How many shelters are there?"

"About twenty. Two are closing soon. No money."

"How many beds?"

"About five thousand."

"And how many homeless?"

"Good question. They're a difficult group to count. Maybe ten thousand."

I thought about that. Then I asked Mordecai about himself. "You have a family?"

"Yes. A wife. Three sons. One's in college, one's in the army. And ... and we lost our third boy on the streets ten years ago. He was killed. Gangs. What about you?"

"Married. No kids."

Mordecai disappeared again. A helper brought cookies. I took four of them and walked to a corner where a young mother was asleep with a baby under her arm and two small children half asleep under blankets.

The oldest boy's eyes opened wide when he saw the cookies in my hand. I gave him one. His eyes shone as he took it and ate all of it. Then he wanted another one. He was small and thin, no more than four years old. The mother woke up, saw the cookies, and smiled.

"What's your name?" I said to the boy. After two cookies he was my friend for life.

"Ontario."

"How old are you?"

He showed me four fingers.

"Four?" I said.

He said yes and put his hand out for another cookie, which I gladly gave him. I wanted to give him things. Anything he wanted.

"Where do you live?" I whispered.

"In a car," he whispered back. "You got more apple juice?"

"Sure." I went to the kitchen and got him a cup of apple juice and more cookies.

The mother was sleeping again. Like many homeless people, she moved a lot in her sleep. She was cold. I took my jacket off and put it over her.

Then the baby cried and woke her. Without thinking, I took the baby, smiling at the mother all the time. She was happy to let me hold it so she could get some sleep. I stayed there until three in the morning.

◆

The next day was Saturday. Since Tuesday, when I met Mister, I hadn't worked even one hour for Drake & Sweeney. I lay in bed. I hated the work at Drake & Sweeney. I didn't want to go back. Ever.

I had breakfast at a café on M and wondered what Ontario was having for breakfast. Then I went shopping. Candy and small toys for the kids, soap for them all, warm clothes in lots of children's sizes. I had never had so much fun spending two hundred dollars. And I wanted to spend more. I wanted to put that family in a hotel for a month. I wanted to start a lawsuit against the person who had made them homeless. I couldn't wait to have Ontario's family as my clients.

I went back to the church, leaving all the toys and clothes in the car, but Ontario's family weren't there. I asked Mordecai where they were.

"Who knows? The homeless go from kitchen to kitchen, shelter to shelter."

◆

Next morning, Sunday, I had the small television in the kitchen on while I ate breakfast. But the TV news stopped me from eating. I heard the words, but I didn't want to believe them. I walked toward the television. My feet were heavy, my heart was cold, my mouth was open in shock and disbelief.

Sometime around 11 P.M., Washington police found a small car near Fort Totten Park, in a gang area in the northeast of the city. It was parked on the street. Inside were a young mother and her children, all dead. The mother had started the engine of the old car and left it running to keep the family warm. The air in the car poisoned them while they slept.

They gave the mother's name. It was Lontae Burton. The baby was Temeko. The other children were Alonzo and Ontario.

Their candy and toys and soap and clothes were still in my car.

CHAPTER 6

A New Person

Now I, too, carried my photograph of a 22-year-old black mother who had died for nothing in a car.

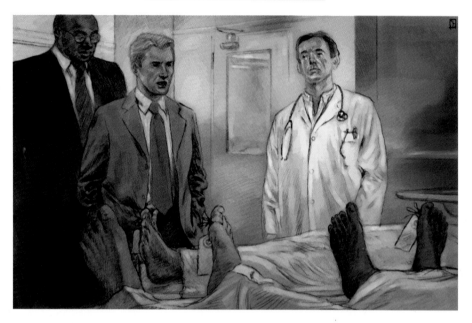

I was at the 14th Street Law Center. "How much would a **funeral** cost?" I asked Mordecai.

"I don't know. Are you interested?"

"I want them to have a good funeral."

"OK, then. Let's arrange it now."

We got into Mordecai's old Ford Taurus. The Burton family's bodies were in the **morgue** of the General Hospital. Mordecai entered like he owned the place.

"I'm Mordecai Green, lawyer for the Burton family," he informed an anxious young man behind the desk.

A doctor from the hospital arrived and Mordecai pushed open the big metal door. Inside the white room were lines of bodies, covered in sheets. Their names were on little pieces of paper tied to their toes.

---

funeral /ˈfyunərəl/ (n) an occasion when people say goodbye to someone who has died
morgue /mɔrg/ (n) a building where dead bodies are kept before they are burned or put in the ground

We stopped in a corner. "Lontae Burton," said the doctor, and pulled the sheet down to her waist. It was Ontario's mother all right, in a white dress. She looked the same as when I saw her alive a few days ago. She looked like she was sleeping. I couldn't stop staring at her.

"That's her," said Mordecai in a confident and loud voice, like he'd known her for years.

Only one sheet covered the children. They were lying in a line with their hands by their sides like little soldiers. I wanted to touch Ontario. I wanted to tell him I was sorry. I wanted to wake him up, take him home, give him some food, give him everything he could ever want.

"That's them," said Mordecai.

I looked up to heaven and I heard a voice in my head say, "Don't let it happen again."

The doctor took us to an office. We helped the assistant make a list of everything that had been found with the family. My old blue jacket was the best thing they owned.

"Do you want it back?" Mordecai asked me.

"No."

I waited outside in the car while Mordecai arranged the funeral in another
office. He told me the price would go up if they saw my expensive clothes. In
lessthan a week I had seen five dead street people. First Mister had changed my
life, now Ontario had broken my heart.

There was a knock on the car window. I jumped. "It's five thousand dollars, all
four," Mordecai shouted through the closed car window.

"Yeah, yeah," I said, and he disappeared back into the hospital.

Soon he was back, driving fast. "The funeral will be Tuesday at the church
here at the hospital. The newspapers will be there. And television. It's a big story."

"Thanks, Mordecai," I said.

"After the funeral, there's going to be a march, a march to the government
buildings on Capitol Hill for the Burton family. Television is going to film it, the
newspapers are going to write about it . . . Are you OK?"

"No."

◆

I called in sick Tuesday. At ten I left for the funeral. It was a very nice church.
Beautiful. It didn't open its doors to the homeless and I could understand why.
I sat alone. I could see Mordecai with two people I didn't know. The TV people
were in one corner.

I could also see the **coffins**. The baby's coffin was very small. Ontario's coffin
and his brother's were bigger, but not much bigger. Lontae Burton's parents were
dead, but her grandmother was there. She put flowers on the coffins and for
a terrible second I thought she was going to open them. I had never been to a
black funeral before and I didn't know what to expect. But I had seen old film of
coffins open at funerals.

After the funeral, there was the march to Capitol Hill. There were big photos of
Lontae Burton everywhere, and under her face the words "WHO KILLED LONTAE?"

On Capitol Hill Mordecai spoke to the people. He didn't talk about the
homeless. He talked about the last hours of the Burton family. He talked about
the baby's last meal, in the church. He talked about the cookies the boys had
eaten.

He described how the little family left the church and went back onto the
streets, into the snowstorm where Lontae and her children lived only a few more
hours. Mordecai described things he didn't actually know had happened, but
I didn't care and the crowd didn't either. When he described the family trying
to get warm before they died, I heard women crying around me. If this man,
Mordecai Green, could make a crowd cry like this, he must be a great lawyer.

coffin /'kɔfɪn/ (n) the box in which a dead person is put

When Mordecai finished we marched to the Capitol, the government building, carrying the coffins. I had never been on a march like this before. Rich people don't march; their world is safe and clean and there are laws to keep them happy. But now I, too, carried my photograph of a 22-year-old black mother who had died for nothing in a car. I wasn't the same person as I had been before Mister and Ontario came into my life, and I could never be that person again.

So I accepted when Mordecai Green phoned me a few days later and invited me to a restaurant near Dupont Circle. And when he invited me to join the 14th Street Law Center, I accepted his offer of a job, too.

"We can pay you thirty thousand dollars a year," smiled Mordecai. "You'll be a partner. Let's see Drake & Sweeney beat that."

I smiled too. I nearly told him about the file I needed from Drake & Sweeney, the file that would give us the story of DeVon Hardy's eviction. But I didn't.

◆

That night, I told Claire my news. It was almost ten and we were sitting in our favorite chairs with glasses of wine. After a few minutes I said, "We need to talk."

"What is it?" she asked, unworried.

"I'm thinking of leaving Drake & Sweeney."

"Oh, really." She either expected this or wanted to seem calm. I had told her all about Lontae Burton and her family.

"Yes, I can't go back there."

"Why not?"

"The work's boring and unimportant. I want to do something to help people. I told you about Mordecai Green. His Law Center has offered me a job. I'm starting Monday."

"How much did he offer you?"

"Thirty thousand a year."

"That's ninety thousand dollars a year less than you earn now."

"You don't do work for the homeless for the money."

As young law and medical students we had wanted to help people. We told ourselves then that money was not important. And now?

"I'm tired," she said. She finished her wine and went to the bedroom.

The next day, she visited a divorce lawyer. I promised to leave the apartment by the weekend.

4.1 Were you right?

Look back at Activity 3.4. Then complete these sentences with *does* or *doesn't*.

1 Michael .... take his father's advice to go back to work.

2 He .... give up working for Drake & Sweeney.

3 He .... spend more time with his wife.

4.2 What more did you learn?

Read this newspaper report about Lontae Burton and her family. Write the missing words.

Family Found Dead in Car

At about 11 P.M. last Saturday night, police found a small ¹ .... on the street near Fort Talbot Park. Inside it were a young black ² .... and three small children. They had left the engine running to keep ³ .... and the gas from the engine had come into the car and killed them while they ⁴ ....

The woman's name was Lontae Burton. Her three children were Temeko (six ⁵ ....), Alonzo (2), and Ontario (⁶ ....). Many of the city's homeless people have suffered recently because ⁷ .... the snowstorms and very cold ⁸ ....

There are only twenty shelters for the ⁹ .... in the whole of the ¹⁰ .... and two of them are closing soon because there is not enough money to keep them ¹¹ .... There are beds for maybe half of the homeless in the shelters and churches, and a few good people ¹² .... hard to organize food and shelter for them on cold nights.

It is ¹³ .... our city did more for its poor and homeless. There will be a ¹⁴ .... next Tuesday after the ¹⁵ .... of the Burton family. Mordecai Green, leader of the 14th Street ¹⁶ .... Center will then give a ¹⁷ .... on Capitol Hill.

.3 Language in use

Look at the sentence on the right. Then write similar sentences. Michael is doing a lot of things for the first time these days.

> **I had never been** on a march like this before.

1 Michael visits a shelter for the homeless.
   Later he says: ..."I had never visited a shelter for the homeless before."...

2 He gives out sandwiches to the hungry.
   He says: ....
   ....

3 He talks to a homeless family.
   He says: ....
   ....

4 He buys clothes and toys for poor children.
   He says: ....
   ....

5 He is suddenly interested in helping the poor.
   He says: ....
   ....

.4 What's next?

Discuss these questions.

1 Michael is going to leave Drake & Sweeney. How can he find out about the eviction if he doesn't work there any longer?
2 What made Claire decide to divorce Michael? Can he save his marriage?

Notes

CHAPTER 7

Braden Chance and RiverOaks

*The note read, "Top key is to Chance's door. Bottom key is
to the file drawer under the window."*

I went back to Drake & Sweeney for my last day. They didn't want me to
leave. There was a lot of work and they didn't want to find someone new. I
was invited to breakfast with Arthur Jacobs in the partners' private dining room
on the eighth floor. How could I turn my back on a world of breakfasts in the
partners' dining room? That was the idea.

Over breakfast, Arthur suggested that I could stop working at Drake &
Sweeney for a year and work *pro bono** at the Law Center. He said that Drake &
Sweeney should do more *pro bono* work. He offered to pay the difference between
the Law Center's thirty thousand a year and what I earned at Drake & Sweeney.

I smiled. I would be Drake & Sweeney's *pro bono* boy for a year and they
could all feel good about themselves. During that year, a partner would take my
clients. I would return after a year, happy, and take my clients back.

Actually, I didn't say no immediately. They had at least tried. Arthur often
talked about *pro bono* work, though clients and their paid hours always came
first. But I thought about the offer and then I said no. By now I hated my old
work too much to go back to it. I didn't like the old me that had done the work
very much, either.

I was trying to explain to Arthur that I was a different man now, when Braden
Chance sat down at a table not far from ours. He didn't see me at first, but then I
saw him staring at me.

"Good morning, Braden," I said loudly.

Arthur turned around to see who I was talking to. "You know him?" he asked
quietly.

"We've met," I said.

"He's a fool," said Arthur, very quietly. It was the same word the legal assistant
had used about Chance.

When I got back to my office, there were two files on my desk. They hadn't
been there before my breakfast with Arthur. In the first one there was a list of
names headed "People Evicted: RiverOaks." Number four was DeVon Hardy.
Number ten was Lontae Burton and three children.

I sat there for two or three minutes in silence. Why would anyone
put something like this on my desk if the information wasn't true? At the

---

* *pro bono* work: work that lawyers do for no money to help people, usually the very poor

36

bottom of the page someone had written a few words in pencil: *The eviction was wrong.*

I opened the second file. There were two keys in it and a typed note. The note read, "Top key is to Chance's door. Bottom key is to the file drawer under the window."

I put the files away. I had to do some work. I also had a working lunch that day. "Working lunch" meant that the client was paying. But the law had never seemed so unimportant and boring. I got through the day only because I knew it was my last at Drake & Sweeney.

It was almost five before I got a few minutes alone. I said goodbye to Polly and locked the office door from the inside. I took the files out again and began to think and make notes. I had an idea who had sent the files: the young legal assistant who had called Chance a fool. Legal assistants did the evictions, and it was his job to put documents in the file.

I phoned another legal assistant and asked him for the name of Chance's assistant. The guy was called Hector Palma. He had been with Drake & Sweeney about three years, all in real estate.

We met in the library on the third floor. Hector Palma was very nervous.

"Did you put those files on my desk?" I asked him. There was no time to play games.

"What files?" His eyes went around and around the room, looking at everything except me.

"The RiverOaks eviction. You were there, right?"

"Yeah," he said.

"What's in the RiverOaks file?"

"Bad stuff."

"Tell me."

"I have a wife and four kids. I need this job."

"You'll be OK."

"You're leaving. What do you care?"

I wasn't surprised he knew. People talked. I was news. "So, before I leave, you want me to go into Chance's office and take a file. And I can't be sure what's in it?"

"Do what you want." And he ran out of the library.

I went back to my office and made some more notes. I would lose my job if I was caught taking the file, but I was already leaving. It would be much worse if I was caught in Chance's office with a key that wasn't mine. I didn't like the idea at all.

Then there was the problem of copying the file. Some Drake & Sweeney files were very thick. I would have to stand in front of a photocopier for a long time.

And also, our photocopiers worked from a plastic card that had our names on it. Drake & Sweeney knew exactly who copied what.

I could use a photocopier somewhere else, but it was illegal to take the file from the building. And I was a lawyer. But couldn't I just borrow the file? I only needed it for half an hour to photocopy it. I could take it to the 14th Street Law Center, photocopy it, and bring it back immediately. That made me a little less of a thief.

It was now getting late, this Friday night. I was starting work with Mordecai on Monday. It was now or never. But I hadn't got a key to the 14th Street Law Center. I looked at my watch. It was half-past six. I drove to 14th Street.

My partners were still there. Sofia actually smiled at me, but only for a second.

"Welcome to your new job," said Mordecai seriously, like I needed all the luck in the world. "How about this," he said, pointing at my new office. "The best office in the area."

"Beautiful," I said, stepping inside. My new office was about half the size of the one I had just left. My Drake & Sweeney desk would be too big to go in there. There was no phone.

"I like it," I said. And I did.

"I'll get you a phone tomorrow," said Mordecai.

It was dark and Sofia wanted to leave. Mordecai and I ate some sandwiches he had bought. He made us both coffee. I looked at the copier. It was about ten years old but I knew it worked.

"What time are you leaving tonight?" I asked Mordecai, with my mouth full of sandwich.

"I don't know. In an hour maybe. Why?"

"I'm going back to Drake & Sweeney for a couple of hours. I have some last minute stuff they want me to finish. Then I'd like to come back here late. Would that be possible?"

Mordecai was eating his sandwich. He reached into a drawer and threw me a key. "Come and go as you please," he said.

"Will it be safe?"

"No. So be careful. Park as close to the door as you can. Walk fast. Then lock yourself in."

I walked fast to my car at seven-thirty. The sidewalk was empty. My Lexus was fine. Maybe I would be OK on the streets.

The drive back to Drake & Sweeney took eleven minutes. If it took thirty minutes to copy Chance's file, then it would be out of his office for about an hour. And he would never know.

Real estate was empty. I knocked on Chance's door. No answer. I used the key to his door and went in. Should I turn on the light? It was dark—I would have to. I locked the door, turned on the light, went to the bottom file drawer under the window and unlocked it with the second key.

I found the RiverOaks file and was reading through it when a voice outside shouted "Hey!" and I jumped. A conversation started outside. Two guys were talking baseball. I turned off the lights, listening to their talk. Then I sat on Chance's sofa for ten minutes.

I could put the file back. If they saw me leaving Chance's office, nothing would be done. It was my last day. But if they saw me taking a file, that was very different. "Be patient," I told myself. After baseball, they started talking about girls. I think they were a couple of young legal assistants, working late. Then, finally, it was quiet.

I locked the drawer in the dark, opened the door, and went out. "Hey!" shouted someone behind me. I ran. I ran to the back of the building, got into the Lexus, and drove off. "That was stupid," I thought. "Why did I run? Why didn't I talk to the guy?" I still worked at Drake & Sweeney, didn't I?

That was my last thought before the Lexus was hit by a Jaguar speeding down 18th Street. I remember a voice saying, "I don't see any blood." And then I remember Claire sitting by my bed at the George Washington University Medical Center.

CHAPTER 8

Hector Palma

"Michael, you won't be a lawyer when they've finished—not here,
not anywhere. You're going to lose your license."

I woke up at seven in the morning and a nurse gave me a note from Claire. It was a really sweet note. It said that she had to go to work and that she had spoken to my doctors and I probably wouldn't die. Claire and I must look like a happily married couple to the doctors and nurses. Why were we getting a divorce?

My left arm was blue. My chest hurt when I breathed. I looked at my face in the bathroom. There were some small cuts, but nothing that wouldn't disappear over the weekend. A nurse told me the Jaguar had been driven by a gang member who sold drugs. "Welcome to the streets," I thought, as I tried not to breathe too much.

The doctor came at seven-thirty. No bones were broken.

They wanted me to stay in hospital for one more day, just to be safe, but I said no.

I had to find a new apartment. The first real estate office sent me to an apartment at Adams-Morgan, north of Dupont Circle. It was three little rooms at the top of a house. Everything in the bathroom worked, the floor was clean, there was a view over the streets. I took it.

That evening I went back to my old apartment to see Claire. We ate a Chinese carryout. Our first ever meal together had been a carryout. And this was our last meal together as husband and wife. Claire had the divorce papers waiting for me on the table and I signed them. In six months I would be single.

"Do you know someone called Hector Palma?" she asked, halfway through the Chinese dinner.

My eyes opened wide. "Yes."

"He called an hour ago. Said he had to talk to you. Who is he?"

"A legal assistant with Drake & Sweeney. He wants me to help him. He has a problem."

"Must be a big one. He wants to meet with you at nine tonight, at Nathan's on M Street."

"Why a bar?" I said, half to myself, half to Claire.

"He didn't say. He sounded strange on the phone."

Suddenly, I wasn't hungry. I finished the meal only because I didn't want to look worried in front of Claire. But it wasn't necessary. She wasn't even looking at me.

I walked to M Street. Parking is impossible on a Saturday night. It was raining and my chest hurt. As I walked, I thought about what to say. I thought of lies

I could tell. After taking the file, it seemed easier to lie. Hector might be there for Drake & Sweeney. He might be **wire**d to record what I said. I would listen carefully and say little.

Nathan's was only half-full. I was ten minutes early but he was there, waiting for me at a table in the corner. As I came in, he jumped up from his seat and put his hand out. "You must be Michael. I'm Hector Palma from real estate. Nice to meet you." Huh? Didn't we meet in the library?

We sat down. He started kicking me under the table. I understood. He was wired and they were watching. A waiter came. I ordered black coffee and Hector asked for a beer.

"I'm a legal assistant in real estate," Hector explained as the drinks arrived. "You've met Braden Chance, one of our partners?"

"Yes," I said. As they were recording everything I said, I would say as little as possible.

"I work mainly for him. You and I spoke for a minute one day last week when you visited his office."

"If you say so. I don't remember seeing you."

wired /waɪəd/ (adj) with recording equipment hidden under your clothes

He smiled and I kicked him back under the table. We both understood the situation now.

"Listen. I asked you to meet me because a file is missing from Braden's office."

"And you think I took it?"

"Well, no, but it could be you. You asked for that file when you went into his office last week."

"So you do think I took it?" I said, angrily. "Well, go to the police."

Hector Palma drank some of his beer. "Drake & Sweeney have already gone to the police," he said. "The police found an empty file in your desk with a note about two keys. One to the door, the other to a file drawer. They also found your **fingerprints** on the file drawer."

I hadn't thought about fingerprints. Drake & Sweeney took everybody's fingerprints when they joined the company. But that was five years ago and I had forgotten about it.

"We might want to speak to you about all this again later," said Hector Palma.

I picked up my coat and left.

◆

fingerprints /ˈfɪŋɡəˌprɪnts/ (n pl) the marks made by the lines at the ends of your fingers

43

I spent my first working day at the 14th Street Law Center getting the file back from the **wreck** of the Lexus. Mordecai helped me. We had to go to Georgia Avenue, where the police keep wrecked cars. I told Mordecai that the file was important but not what was in it.

Back home in my new apartment, I looked at the file. RiverOaks was a real estate company. They wanted to build a new mail office for the Washington Post Office and then rent the building to them. They had bought the warehouse where DeVon Hardy and Lontae Burton lived and they wanted to pull it down and start rebuilding.

They were in a hurry. They wanted to start pulling the warehouse down in February. On January 27, Hector Palma visited the warehouse. His note about that visit was on the list of documents in the file, but it wasn't actually in the file. Somebody had taken it out, almost certainly Chance, after Mister had visited us.

wreck /rek/ (n/v) a car that cannot be repaired because it is so damaged

On Friday January 31, Hector Palma returned to the warehouse, with the police, and evicted the people who were living there. The eviction had taken three hours. Hector Palma's note about it was two pages long. Although he tried to hide what he felt, it was clear that he disliked being part of the eviction.

He described how Lontae Burton had fought with the police. My heart stopped when I read: *The mother had three children, one, a baby. She lived in a two-room apartment with no bathroom. They slept on the floor. She fought with the policemen while her children watched. In the end she was carried out of the building.*

I drove to 14th Street and copied the file. Then I went back to my old apartment. Claire was at the hospital. I took my sleeping bag, a few suits, my radio, the small TV from the kitchen, my CD player and a few CDs, a coffeepot, a hair dryer, and three blue towels.

I left a note telling her I was gone. I didn't know what I felt. I had never moved out before; I wasn't sure how it was done. As I drove away, I didn't feel happy to be single again. Claire and I had both lost.

Back at the 14th Street Law Center, my first visitor was my old friend Barry Nuzzo. He sat down carefully in the chair opposite my desk—he didn't want to get dirt on his expensive suit. Was he wired, like Hector Palma? Maybe they had sent Barry because he was my friend and also one of Mister's guests that Tuesday afternoon.

"So you're here for the money?" he said. Joke.

"Of course."

"You're crazy. They're going to come after you, Michael. You can't take a file."

"You mean a criminal lawsuit for **theft**?"

"Probably. And they talked to the Bar Association.* Rafter's working on it. Michael, you won't be a lawyer when they've finished—not here, not anywhere. You're going to lose your **license**."

I wasn't ready for that. "I have the file. The file has plenty of information about Drake & Sweeney in it."

"You can't use the file, Michael. You can't use it in a lawsuit because you took it from our offices and that's theft."

I said nothing. I didn't know what I was going to do. But I knew I couldn't give the file back now. I had nothing else in the fight against Drake & Sweeney. Barry stood up to leave.

"Will you phone me some time, Michael?" he said, at the door.

"Sure."

* Bar Association: a professional group for lawyers which gives lawyers their license

theft /θeft/ (n) the crime of stealing something
license /ˈlaɪsəns/ (n) an official document that gives you permission to do something

5.1 Were you right?

Look back at Activity 4. 4. Then answer these questions, *Yes* or *No*.

1 Do the partners at Drake & Sweeney want Michael to leave? ....

2 Do they want to stop him doing *pro bono* work? ....

3 Does Arthur Jacobs have a good opinion of Braden Chance? ....

4 Does Hector Palma help Michael? ....

5 Did the Burton family live in the same warehouse as DeVon Hardy? ....

5.2 What more did you learn?

Put these events in the right order. Number them, 1–8.

1 ☐ Michael takes the RiverOaks file from Chance's office.

2 ☐ Michael has a meeting with Palma in Nathan's bar.

3 ☐ Michael is hurt in a car crash.

4 1 Someone puts keys to Chance's office on Michael's desk.

5 ☐ Michael's friend, Barry, tells him that Drake & Sweeney know that he has stolen the RiverOaks file.

6 ☐ Michael finds a new apartment.

7 ☐ Michael goes to the 14th Street Law Center and gets a key to it from Mordecai.

8 ☐ Michael gets the file from his car and copies it.

3.3 Language in use

Look at the sentence on the right, a report of Claire's note. Then write reports of these notes in the same way.

> The note from Claire **said that she had to** go to work and that **she had spoken** to my doctors and I probably **wouldn't die**.

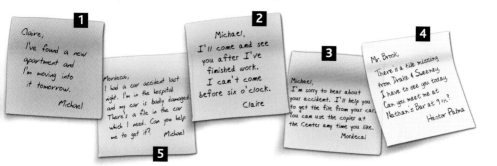

1

Claire,
I've found a new apartment and I'm moving into it tomorrow.
Michael

2

Michael,
I'll come and see you after I've finished work.
I can't come before six o'clock.
Claire

Mordecai,
I had a car accident last night. I'm in the hospital and my car is badly damaged. There's a file in the car which I need. Can you help me to get it? Michael

3

Michael,
I'm sorry to hear about your accident. I'll help you to get the file from your car. You can use the copier at the Center any time you like.
Mordecai

4

Mr. Brock,
There's a file missing from Drake & Sweeney. I have to see you today. Can you meet me at Nathan's Bar at 9 pm?
Hector Palma

5

1 Michael's note said that he had found a new appartment and he was moving into it the next/following morning.

2 ....

3 ....

4 ....

5 ....

4 What's next?

Discuss these questions. Who has done something illegal? What have they done?

| Michael | Hector Palma | Braden Chance |
| Drake & Sweeney | RiverOaks Real Estate Company | |

CHAPTER 9

The Homeless

"I'm Michael. Where do you live, Ruby?"
"Here and there."

The building had been a department store, many years ago. Now the sign on it said SAMARITAN HOUSE.

"It's a private shelter," Mordecai said. "Ninety beds. The food's OK. Some churches in Arlington got together and they pay for everything. We've been coming here for six years."

Inside we used a bedroom as an office. "This is a good office," Mordecai said. "We can be private here."

"What about a bathroom?" I asked.

"They're in the back. You don't get your own bathroom in a shelter."

I could hear radios. People were getting up. It was Monday morning and they had jobs to go to.

"Is it easy to get a room here?" I asked Mordecai, although I already knew the answer.

"Nearly impossible. There's a long waiting list."

"How long do they stay?"

"Maybe three months. This is one of the nicer shelters, so they're safe here. After three months the shelter tries to find them an apartment."

"And our clients all come from shelters?" I asked.

"Half come from the shelters," Mordecai said. "The other half from the streets."

"We take anybody?"

"Anybody who's homeless. The people here at this shelter have jobs, but they don't earn enough to pay rent for an apartment. So when they get one, they lose it again. One missed paycheck and they lose their homes."

My first client was called Waylene, age twenty-seven, two children, no husband. Her problem wasn't complicated. She had worked in a fast-food restaurant. She started to tell us why she left her job, but Mordecai said that the reason didn't matter. She hadn't had her last two paychecks. Because she had no address, the restaurant had sent the checks to the wrong place. The checks had disappeared, and nobody at the restaurant cared.

"Will you be here next week?" Mordecai asked.

Waylene wasn't sure. Maybe here, maybe there. She was looking for a job, she might move in with someone. Or get her own apartment.

"We'll get your money and we'll have the checks sent to our office," said Mordecai. He gave her the address of the 14th Street Law Center. She said "thanks" and left.

"Call the fast-food restaurant," Mordecai told me. "Tell them you're Waylene's lawyer. Be nice at first. If they don't send the checks, stop being nice. If necessary, go there and get the checks yourself."

I wrote down everything Mordecai said, like it was complicated. Waylene's paychecks were for two hundred and ten dollars. My last client at Drake & Sweeney was trying to get nine hundred million dollars. But I was happy enough when I got home at the end of the day.

◆

My new apartment now had some old chairs in it, and the TV was on a box. I smiled at my furniture. My mother had called. I listened to her voice on the answerphone. She and Dad wanted to visit me.

That evening I watched basketball on TV and had a few beers. At eleven-thirty I called Claire. We hadn't talked in four days. Why shouldn't we talk? We were actually still married. I thought maybe we could have dinner soon.

The phone rang and then a voice said, "Hello?" It was a man. I couldn't speak. I had been gone less than a week and Claire had a man in the apartment at eleven-thirty. I almost put the phone down, but then I said, "I'd like to speak to Claire, please."

"Who's calling?"

"Michael, her husband."

"She's in the shower," he said. He sounded pleased with himself.

"Tell her I called," I said.

I walked around the room until midnight, then I went for a walk in the cold. Why did our marriage go wrong? Who was that guy? Was he someone she had known for years and I didn't know about him? I told myself it didn't matter. We weren't divorcing because of other people. We were divorcing because of us. And if she was free to find another guy, then I was free to find someone too. Yeah, right.

At 2 A.M. I was walking around Dupont Circle, stepping over people sleeping in the street. It was dangerous, but I didn't care. After a couple of hours, I went home and got some sleep. Then I wanted to work. I got to 14th Street before eight that morning, ready to start.

As I walked through the snow, making my way to the Law Center, I thought of my clients. By now I had a few. There was Waylene and her paychecks.

There was also Marvis. Like me, Marvis wanted a divorce. His wife was on drugs. She had taken everything he had, including their two children. Marvis wanted them back.

"How long will a divorce take?" Marvis had asked me.

"Six months," I told him.

Marvis was clean, he didn't drink, and he was looking for work. I enjoyed the half hour I spent with him and I wanted to help him.

Another client was a 58-year-old woman. Her husband was dead and the government was sending her money to the wrong place. I could get all her money back and then get it sent to the right place.

A lot of my clients had problems like that. They were just not getting money, often from the government, that should be theirs.

When I reached the Law Center, a little woman was sitting against our door. The office was still locked. It was below freezing in the streets. When she saw me, she jumped to her feet and said, "Good morning, are you a lawyer?"

"Yes, I am."

"For people like me?"

She looked like she was homeless. "Sure. Come in." I opened the door. It was colder inside than outside. I made some coffee and found some old cookies. I offered them to her and she quickly ate one.

"What's your name?" I asked. We were sitting in the front office, next to Sofia's desk, waiting for the coffee and for the office to get a little warmer.

"Ruby," she said.

"I'm Michael. Where do you live, Ruby?"

"Here and there." She was between thirty and forty, dressed in a lot of old clothes. She was very thin.

"Tell me," I said, "I need to know. Do you live in a shelter?"

"Not now," she said. "I live in a car. I sleep in the back."

I poured two large paper cups full of coffee and we went into my office. "What can I do for you?" I asked.

With both hands on the coffee cup, to keep warm, and without looking at me, she told me her story. She and her son Terence lived in a small apartment. When Terence was about ten, she went to prison for four months for selling drugs. Terence lived with her sister those four months, but when Ruby came out of prison they had lost the apartment. She and Terence slept in cars, warehouses, and under bridges in warm weather. When it was cold, they went to the shelters. She couldn't stop taking drugs.

A few years back she had worked for a couple called Rowlands. Their children were grown and away from home. Ruby offered to pay Mr. and Mrs. Rowlands fifty dollars a month if Terence could stay with them. The Rowlands weren't sure at first, but in the end they agreed.

Terence had a small bedroom at the Rowlands' house. He started to get good grades at school. The Rowlands were good people. Ruby was allowed to visit Terence for an hour each night. With great difficulty, she managed to pay each month as agreed. She was pleased with herself.

Until she went to prison again. She couldn't stop taking drugs. And now Terence didn't want to talk to her. He wanted to join the army—Mr. Rowlands was an army man. One night Ruby took some drugs and then went to the Rowlands' house. She screamed and shouted and the Rowlands and Terence threw her out.

The next day the Rowlands started a lawsuit. They wanted Terence to become their son. Ruby wasn't allowed to visit him until she stopped taking drugs.

"I want to see my son," she said. "I miss him so bad."

"You won't see Terence until you stop the drugs," I said, trying to say it nicely. I had to get her onto a drugs program.

Sofia knew where Ruby should go. Sofia knew everything and everybody. She made a phone call and then Ruby and I were on our way to Naomi's Women's Center on 10th Street. It opened at seven, closed at four, and between those hours helped women with a drug problem.

I spoke with Megan, the young woman in charge of Naomi's. We had a long talk. It was the first long talk I had had with anyone in a long time.

CHAPTER 10

Chicago

"There's going to be a lawsuit, Hector," I said. "Against Drake & Sweeney. You can't hide from that."

I was sleeping on the floor at the apartment. I liked it down there and it helped me understand my new clients. In the middle of the night, the phone rang. It was Claire. The police were in her apartment, wanting to search it for the file. I looked at my watch. It was 1 A.M. "I'll be right there."

The door was open and I ran in. There were three policemen in there and I shouted at the nearest one. "I'm Michael Brock. Who are you?"

"**Lieutenant** Gasko," said the policeman, not very nicely.

"Claire," I shouted. "Get the video camera. There's going to be a lawsuit, Lieutenant Gasko."

lieutenant /luˈtɛnənt/ (n) a title for a police officer

Lieutenant Gasko showed me a document. "It's signed by a judge," he said. "And it says we can search for the file." But he knew I was a lawyer and he didn't look very happy.

"The file's not here because I don't live here," I said. "Now give me your names and then go."

Claire was filming it all with the video camera. Their document was fine and I knew that. But the three policemen gave me their names and then left.

"Can they come back?" asked Claire.

"No."

"That's good."

"Did you tell them where I live?" I asked her.

"Michael, I don't know where you live. You just gave me a phone number."

I said goodnight without touching or kissing her. I knew that was what she wanted.

I thought hard. Now I had to tell Mordecai everything. It was possible that the police would come to the Law Center, looking for the file.

◆

Next morning I tried to phone Hector Palma from the Law Center. His secretary said he had left the Washington office. I put the phone down. Now what? I stared at the ceiling.

Mordecai came into my office. I started my story: "My wife and I aren't together. I moved out of our apartment."

"I'm sorry," said Mordecai. What else could he say?

"Don't be. Early this morning, the police tried to search the apartment where I used to live. They were looking for a file that I took when I left Drake & Sweeney."

"What kind of file?"

"The DeVon Hardy and Lontae Burton file."

"I'm listening."

"I don't think that DeVon Hardy and Lontae Burton and the others were squatters. I think they were tenants. And if they were tenants, the eviction was illegal."

"It sure was. Can't evict tenants without warning. But do you know? Or are you guessing?"

I told Mordecai the story of the RiverOaks file. I told him that something, probably a note dated January 27, was missing from the file.

"And what do you think is in this note?" he asked.

"I can't be sure. But I think it's a note from Hector Palma. I think he knew they were tenants and he said that in the note. But RiverOaks wanted them out quickly so they could start pulling the warehouse down. They wanted to start the new building for the Post Office in February. I think Hector Palma's note of January 27 was removed from the file so Drake & Sweeney could evict DeVon Hardy and Lontae Burton and the others as squatters."

"Good," said Mordecai. "So we start a lawsuit for the family of Lontae Burton and the other people who were evicted."

"Yes," I said. "That way, Hector Palma has to tell the judge what he knows."

"I'll contact Lontae Burton's parents," Mordecai said. "They would be our clients in the lawsuit."

"Her parents are dead. But she has a grandmother."

"Fine. She'll be our client. But first we need to find Hector Palma."

"I think Drake & Sweeney will keep him in the company. If he leaves the company, they lose control of him. But they want him out of Washington. I think he's working for Drake & Sweeney in another city. Probably a new job with more money."

"Sofia!" shouted Mordecai, loud enough to be heard on Capitol Hill. "Sofia, we're looking for someone."

Sofia came in with paper and a pencil. "I know," she said. "I heard." She turned to me. "I can help. Tell me everything you know about this person."

I told Sofia Hector Palma's name, address, and job. I described him and said he had a wife and four kids.

"Age?"

"Maybe thirty."

"How much did he get a month at Drake & Sweeney?"

"As a legal assistant? Three thousand."

"He has four kids, so one or more will be in school. He can't send kids to a private school on thirty-five thousand. We'll start with the schools. Then the churches."

She went back to her desk and she was on the phone for an hour. Each time she said hello in English, asked for the person she wanted, and then the conversation was in Spanish.

An hour later she came back into my office. "They moved to Chicago. Do you need an address?"

"But how did you . . . ?"

"Don't ask. A friend of a friend in their church. They moved to Chicago last weekend. I can get you an address but it will take longer."

"I don't need an address. I've been to Drake & Sweeney's Chicago office a couple of times."

◆

Two days later I was there again. But I hadn't flown first class, as in the old days. I waited outside the Drake & Sweeney building from seven in the morning while 106 lawyers—the third highest number after Washington and New York—arrived for work.

At 8:20, Hector Palma arrived and I followed him into the building. He got off on floor number fifty-one. There was a phone there. I phoned Mordecai and told him about my progress. Then I phoned Megan at Naomi's Women's Center. Ruby was still there, doing OK. Hector Palma wasn't going anywhere for the next ten hours, so I had another long talk with Megan.

There was a list of partners' names on each floor. I chose one. "I have an appointment with Dick Heile," I said loudly as I passed the desk. And then I walked past the desk, down the hall.

Hector had his own office in Chicago.

"Hello, Hector," I said as I walked in. "So how's Chicago?"

"What ... What are you doing here?"

I sat on Hector's desk. "There's going to be a lawsuit, Hector," I said. "Against Drake & Sweeney. You can't hide from that."

I didn't feel as confident as I tried to sound.

"And who's starting this lawsuit?"

"Lontae Burton's grandmother. And later the other people who were evicted, when we find them."

Hector just looked at me.

"You remember Lontae, don't you, Hector? She was the young mother who fought with the policemen when you were evicting everyone. You felt bad about it because you knew she was a tenant. So you wrote that in a note, dated January 27 and you put that in the file. But Braden Chance took your note out again. That's why I'm here, Hector. I want a copy of that note."

"Why would I have a copy?"

"Because you're smart, Hector. You knew that Drake & Sweeney's evictions were illegal. You knew how important your note was. Maybe you even guessed Braden Chance would remove it."

Hector thought about that. I guessed he wouldn't be happy hiding in Chicago. The evictions were wrong and he knew it. He had tried to help me once before. "Meet me at twelve in front of the building," he said.

He was there on time. "I have four children, please protect me," he said, as he gave me an envelope. I thanked him, got a taxi, and opened the envelope.

The note was dated January 27. It said that the tenants were paying one hundred dollars a month rent on the fifteenth of every month to man called Johnny. There was even a copy of a **receipt** signed by Johnny, saying that he had received one hundred dollars rent from Lontae Burton on January 15. It couldn't be any clearer. They were tenants. The eviction was illegal.

At Chicago O' Hare airport I **fax**ed copies of the note and the receipt to Mordecai. Then I caught the next plane back to Washington. A taxi from the airport took me back to 14th Street, where Mordecai and Sofia weren't looking as happy as I had expected. Lieutenant Gasko was in the office, waiting for me.

As he took me out to the police car, Sofia was phoning fast and talking fast, first in English, then in Spanish. But she and Mordecai couldn't stop Lieutenant Gasko taking me to Central Police Station like any other criminal. Drake & Sweeney said I had taken their file, and that was theft.

---

receipt /rɪˈsiːt/ (n) a piece of paper that shows you have received something

fax /fæks/ (v) to send a document electronically down a telephone line to a machine that prints it

CHAPTER 11

Megan

Her eyes held mine for a second and I thought,
"no wedding ring on her finger."

It was Friday afternoon. I knew Mordecai could get me out on **bail**, but some very bad things could happen to a good-looking white boy in prison over the weekend.

In the police car to Central, I tried to think about all the great people who had spent some time in prison—like Martin Luther King. But then I thought of my parents. Their son in prison would be the end of their world. My friends already thought I had ruined my life. I didn't know what Claire would think, especially as she had a new man now.

At Central, Gasko led me like a lost dog. They took everything I had in my pockets and I signed for it. Then my photograph and fingerprints were taken. There were police everywhere but only one other white face—a man who was very drunk.

We were walking to the **cell**s. I was scared. "Can I get bail?" I asked.

"I think your lawyer's working on it," Gasko said.

The cell door closed behind me. There were five other prisoners in the cell with me, all black, all much younger than me. I sat on the floor.

In the cell opposite, I could see the drunk white guy and hear him shouting. Two large black men had him in a corner of the cell. They were hitting his head. Minutes passed. One of the young guys in my cell walked over to me. This was the end.

"Nice jacket," he said, touching my jacket with his foot as I sat on the floor.

"Thanks," I said, trying to sound like I meant it.

He was eighteen or nineteen. Thin. Probably a gang member who had spent his life on the streets. "I could use a jacket like that," he said, giving me a kick with his foot.

"You shouldn't be a low-life street gang member then," I thought. "Would you like to borrow the jacket?" I asked. I wasn't going to fight back. If I did, the other four would help the first one.

"What did you say?"

"I said, 'Would you like to borrow . . .'"

The kick caught me in the head and I shouted from the shock.

bail /beɪl/ (n) money that buys someone's freedom until they have to return to a court of law
cell /sel/ (n) a small room in a prison or a police station

59

"My friend said he could use a jacket like that," said one of the other four. "A gift would be nice."

I quickly took off my jacket and held it toward the young gang member who had kicked me.

"Is this a gift?" he said, taking it.

"It's whatever you want it to be."

He kicked me again, hard in the head. "Is this a gift?"

"Yes."

"Thanks, man."

I sat in a ball on the floor. My face hurt. The floor was getting cold. What would happen when I needed the toilet?

"Nice shoes," said a voice above me. I gave them to him.

Mordecai got me out on bail at 7 P.M. My bail was ten thousand dollars.

◆

My friends at Drake & Sweeney had told the newspapers about my stay in prison. *Lawyer out on bail. Was it theft?* I read, the next day. They took a photo of me when I first joined Drake & Sweeney and that was there too. They were trying to ruin my life. I wondered which client was paying for all the hours Rafter and Arthur Jacobs were spending on me. A client was definitely paying. A client paid for every hour of every lawyer's time. RiverOaks, probably.

I went in to work at 14th Street. Ruby was asleep in front of the door.

"Why are you sleeping here?" I asked. She didn't answer. She was hungry. I unlocked the door, made coffee, and went to find the cookies.

The phone rang. It was Megan. Ruby had left Naomi's.

"Are you taking drugs again?" I asked Ruby.

She didn't look at me. "No," she said.

"Yes, you are. Don't lie to me, Ruby. I'm your friend and your lawyer and I'll help you see Terence. But I can't help if you lie to me. Now will you go back to Naomi's?"

"Yes."

"Good. I'll take you."

"OK." She took another cookie, her fourth.

On the way back to Naomi's, she said, "You were in prison."

"How did you know?"

"You hear stuff on the street."

When we arrived, Megan took Ruby into the women's group and then asked me to stay for coffee. She threw a Washington Post to me. "Bad night, huh?" she said with a smile.

There was my photo again. "It wasn't too bad."

"What's this?" she asked, pointing at my face.

"A guy in my cell wanted my shoes. He took them."

She looked at my shoes. Old Nikes. "Those?"

"Yes. Good shoes, aren't they?"

"How long were you in there?"

"A couple of hours. Then I got my life together. I'm a new man now."

She smiled again, a perfect smile. Her eyes held mine for a second and I thought, "No wedding ring on her finger." She was tall and a little too thin. Her hair was dark red and short and well-cut. Her eyes were light brown, very big and round, and nice to look at. She was very attractive and I wondered why I hadn't noticed it before.

I told her about me. She told me about herself. Her father was in the church in Maryland. He liked baseball and he loved Washington. As a teenager, Megan had decided to work with the poor. It was a job—but a job she liked.

I told her the story of Mister and how I had started working with the homeless. She was very interested and asked lots of questions. Then she asked me to come back later for lunch. If the sun was shining, we could eat outside. I liked that. I thought it was romantic. You can find love anywhere, even in a shelter for homeless women.

6.1 Were you right?

Look at the questions in Activity 5.4 again. Complete these sentences.

1 Michael has taken a .... from the Drake & Sweeney building.

2 Hector Palma gave Michael .... to Chance's room and file drawer.

3 Braden Chance allowed the eviction of people who were ...., not squatters.

4 Chance is a partner in Drake & Sweeney, so they are .... for his actions.

5 RiverOaks Real Estate Company evicted people illegally from a .... that they wanted to pull down quickly.

6.2 What more did you learn?

1 Michael has some new clients at the 14th Street Law Center. Make sentences about them.

Michael has a client	whose wife is on drugs.	His name is	Marvis.
	who wants a divorce.		Ruby.
	who can't see her son until she stops taking drugs.	Her name is	Waylene.
	who used to work in a fast-food restaurant.		

2 Are these sentences right (✓) or wrong (✗)?

a ☐ The police search Claire's apartment for the missing file.

b ☐ The file has a note in it from Hector Palma.

c ☐ Hector Palma doesn't work for Drake & Sweeney now.

d ☐ In Chicago, Hector Palma gives Michael a copy of his note.

e ☐ Michael is kept in a police cell over the weekend.

f ☐ The other prisoners beat him and steal his jacket and shoes.

g ☐ Megan is in a Women's Center because she takes drugs.

5.3 Language in use

Look at the sentences on the right. Then make similar sentences from each pair of sentences below. Use *without* and an *-ing* verb form.

> **Without looking** at me, she told me her story.
>
> I said goodnight **without touching** or **kissing** her.

1 Waylene left her job at the restaurant. She didn't give them an address.

   Waylene left her job at the restaurant without giving them an address.

2 The police came into Claire's apartment. They didn't warn her.

3 The police didn't find anything. They left the apartment.

4 RiverOaks didn't want to wait for a legal eviction. They pulled the warehouse down.

5 Michael didn't make an appointment. He just walked into Palma's office.

Now join these sentences with *before* or *after* and an *–ing* verb form.

6 Michael spent several hours in a police cell. Then he got out on bail.

7 The men kicked Michael in the head. Then they stole his jacket and shoes.

5.4 What's next?

How do you think the story will end? Talk to other students.

CHAPTER 12

The Washington Post

*The photographs said it all. Because of Drake & Sweeney,
these poor people were dead.*

The file was thick; Rafter had worked very hard. It was my copy of Drake &
Sweeney's complaint to the Bar Association. In one sentence: I had stolen
their file, so now I should lose my license.

But it was a shock. Drake & Sweeney wanted blood, my blood. It was
frightening. Since I had started law school ten years earlier, I had never thought
of any other kind of work. What would I do without a law license?

But there was one thing Drake & Sweeney didn't know yet. Tomorrow
morning at nine o'clock, Mordecai and I were starting a four million dollar
lawsuit against them for the death of the Burton family.

I went into Mordecai's office. "What do I do?" I said.

He smiled. "Same as they did. Call the *Washington Post*. I was at college with Tim Claussen. He's one of their best journalists."

Next morning we told Tim Claussen about the lawsuit against Drake & Sweeney. The Burton story was already big as a result of the march and my night in prison, and this made it even bigger. He asked us a lot of questions and I was happy to answer. Drake & Sweeney went to the newspapers first.

The story was in the newspaper the next day. For an old law company like Drake & Sweeney, it was the worst thing in the world. Arthur Jacobs's photo appeared next to DeVon Hardy's. There were also photographs of Lontae Burton taken from the march. You didn't even have to read the story; the photographs said it all. Because of Drake & Sweeney, these poor people were dead.

The next day it got even worse for Drake & Sweeney. The Post Office didn't like all these stories in the newspapers and they didn't want RiverOaks as their real estate company. That left RiverOaks with nothing. RiverOaks told the *Washington Post* they didn't know the evictions were illegal. A million dollar lawsuit for lost business by RiverOaks against Drake & Sweeney was becoming possible.

◆

Arthur Jacobs phoned Mordecai at the Law Center. He wanted to meet Mordecai at Drake & Sweeney's offices to talk about the lawsuit. Without me. Mordecai smiled at me. "This could be the meeting," he said.

"Maybe," I replied.

My future could depend on Mordecai's talk with Arthur Jacobs. That night I couldn't sleep. Mordecai was enjoying himself. He told me afterward that he couldn't believe Arthur Jacobs was nearly eighty.

The old man told Mordecai immediately that Braden Chance was gone. He didn't choose to leave Drake & Sweeney. They told him to go. Chance had been the only one who knew those people were tenants. I believed that.

Mordecai showed Arthur Jacobs the missing note from the file, and the receipt. Rafter was at the meeting too, with some other lawyers, and for a long time none of them said a word.

Then Arthur Jacobs made a suggestion: he said he wanted to meet with us and a judge. With the judge there, we could decide everything on one day—the Burton lawsuit, the theft of the file lawsuit, and the Bar Association complaint. The judge would be Judge DeOrio, who Mordecai knew was a fair judge.

"What do you think?" Mordecai asked me.

"What do *you* think?"

"I say we do it. I'll call Judge DeOrio and arrange a time."

CHAPTER 13

Burton Against Drake & Sweeney

*"You put this family on the street. You've told us you did.
And that's where they died."*

We were in Judge DeOrio's room, but this wasn't a court. There were two lawyers from RiverOaks. From Drake & Sweeney there was Arthur Jacobs, Rafter, Nathan Malamud, and Barry Nuzzo. Why Malamud and Nuzzo, who were not going to speak for Drake & Sweeney? Then I understood. Malamud and Nuzzo had gone back to work after that Tuesday with Mister. They were fine. So why wasn't I?

Judge DeOrio said good morning and then gave Mordecai five minutes to make the complaint against Drake & Sweeney in the Burton lawsuit. Mordecai needed just two minutes. He explained clearly how Drake & Sweeney's illegal eviction led to the deaths of Lontae Burton and her children.

Arthur Jacobs spoke for Drake & Sweeney. He didn't disagree with Mordecai about what had happened to Lontae and her children. But he said it was, in part, her own fault.

"There were places for her to go," Arthur said. "There were shelters open. She spent the night before in a church, with many other people. Why did she leave? Her grandmother has an apartment in Northeast. Why didn't this mother do more to protect her little family?"

"Why was she in the street at all?" DeOrio asked, and I almost smiled.

Arthur stayed calm. "The eviction was wrong," he said. "We are not arguing with Mr. Green about that. We are saying that events after the eviction were partly the mother's fault."

"How much of it was her fault?" asked Judge DeOrio.

"At least half."

"That's too high."

"We don't agree, Judge DeOrio."

"Mr. Green?"

Mordecai stood, shaking his head in disbelief, like Arthur was a first-year law student. "These people have nowhere to live, Mr. Jacobs. That's why they're called homeless. You put this family on the street. You've told us you did. And that's where they died. We could go to court. Would you say the same thing there? Stand up in court, Mr. Jacobs! Say, 'It was the mother's fault her family died.'"

Arthur and the rest of the Drake & Sweeney lawyers looked scared enough at the idea of telling a court full of black people that the Burton family's death was, in part, Lontae's fault.

"Drake & Sweeney are guilty of an illegal eviction," said Judge DeOrio. "That's clear. I wouldn't advise you to blame the mother in a court."

Mordecai and Arthur sat down. We had won the Burton lawsuit without going to court. Now we would discuss how much Drake & Sweeney should pay. Rafter stood up. He talked about how much money you usually got for dead children in lawsuits. He had read a lot of these lawsuits across the US. He offered fifty thousand dollars for each child. He became boring. He started to discuss the amount of money Lontae had lost because she died and so she didn't go to work. That was added to the money you usually got for dead children. In total, he offered seven hundred and seventy thousand dollars.

"Is that your final offer, Mr. Rafter?" asked Judge DeOrio. He looked like he hoped it wasn't.

"No, sir," Rafter said.

"Mr. Green."

Mordecai stood again. "We do not accept their offer, Judge DeOrio. Sir, this talk of the value of each child means nothing to me. I know how much I can get if this comes to court and the people of Washington decide. And that is a lot more than Mr. Rafter is offering. These children were, of course, homeless black children. Mr. Rafter, you have a son at private school. Would you take fifty thousand dollars for him?"

Rafter looked down and didn't reply.

"I can walk into a Washington court and I can get a million dollars each for Lontae Burton's little children. That's the same as any child in an expensive school in Virginia or Maryland."

The defense team looked at each other. They all had kids in expensive schools in Virginia and Maryland. Mordecai then talked about the last hours of Lontae Burton and her family, as he had at Capitol Hill. He was a born storyteller and he had a good story to tell. His voice went up and then down in anger. At the end he pointed at the Drake & Sweeney lawyers, speaking for them. "Those people in that warehouse," he shouted. "They're just a bunch of squatters. Throw them out!"

He asked for four million dollars. It was silent in the room when he finished. Judge DeOrio made some notes. The next thing to discuss was the file.

"Do you have the file?" Judge DeOrio asked me.

"Yes, sir."

"Will you give it to me?"

"Yes, sir."

Mordecai gave Judge DeOrio the file and we all sat and watched for ten minutes while the judge read it. When he had finished he said, "The file has been returned, Mr. Jacobs. There was a criminal lawsuit about its theft. What do you want to do now?"

"If we can agree on the Burton lawsuit, we will stop the criminal lawsuit against Mr. Brock for theft of the file."

"Mr. Brock? Is that acceptable to you?"

Yes! "Yes, sir. It is."

"Next, we have the complaint to the Bar Association by Drake & Sweeney against Michael Brock. Mr. Jacobs?"

Arthur stood up again. He talked about why it was wrong for a lawyer to steal a file from his own company. He didn't seem to be enjoying it, and he didn't take too long about it. But I had been one of them and then I had damaged them. They wouldn't forgive me for that. The complaint to the Bar Association wouldn't be stopped.

I wasn't a criminal, Arthur said, so they would stop the theft lawsuit. But I was a lawyer and a good one. And so the complaint should go to the Bar Association.

The lawyers from RiverOaks didn't speak, but it was clear they agreed. It was, of course, their client's file I had taken. And Arthur spoke so well that actually I agreed with him too.

"Mr. Brock?" said Judge DeOrio. "Do you have anything to say?"

I hadn't prepared anything, but I wasn't afraid to say what I felt. I looked Arthur in the eyes and said, "Mr. Jacobs, I have always had a very high opinion of you, and I still do. I was wrong to take the file and I am sorry I did it. I was looking for information and I was going to put the file back, but all that is no excuse. I apologize to you, to Drake & Sweeney, and to your client, RiverOaks."

Mordecai told me afterwards that he knew immediately Drake & Sweeney would agree to his next suggestion. The anger had gone out of the situation.

Mordecai suggested twenty-five thousand dollars each to all the people evicted by Drake & Sweeney, when we could find them. He suggested three million dollars for the Burton lawsuit, paid at three hundred thousand a year. And after a lot of talk, we agreed that I would lose my license for nine months only.

CHAPTER 14

A New Life

"I'm thinking about my new life," I said.
And we both smiled.

Early Friday I was happily helping homeless people at the 14th Street Law Center, though not, of course, speaking as a lawyer, when Arthur Jacobs suddenly appeared at my door. I said hello nicely, though I couldn't imagine what he wanted. He said no to coffee. He just wanted to talk.

Arthur said that the last few weeks had been the most difficult of his fifty-six years as a lawyer. Drake & Sweeney was OK again now, but he still couldn't sleep. He felt guilty about the deaths of the Burton family and he would never forget it. And he was tired of chasing money. I was too surprised to say much, so I just listened. Arthur was suffering and I felt sorry for him.

He asked about the Law Center and the work we did. How long had the Center been there? How many people worked there? Where did the money come from? This gave me an opportunity and I took it. I told Arthur that because I couldn't work as a lawyer, I was starting a *pro bono* program. I was going to use lawyers from the big Washington law companies. These volunteer lawyers would work a few hours a week and I would tell them what to do. We could reach thousands of homeless people.

Arthur liked the idea. As we discussed it, the program grew larger. After a few minutes, he was talking about sending all 400 of his Washington lawyers to do *pro bono* work for a few hours a week.

"Would 400 lawyers be too many?" Arthur asked.

"No," I said. "But I'll need help from inside Drake & Sweeney. I know someone. He's at the Chicago office, but I'm sure you can get him back."

As I had guessed, Arthur knew nothing about Hector Palma or how he had helped me get the RiverOaks file. Hector would be back in Washington in a month, working with me.

Arthur stayed in my office for two hours. He was a much happier man when he left. He had a purpose in life. I walked him to his car and then ran to tell Mordecai the good news. We could help as many homeless people as we needed to.

◆

Megan's uncle owned a house near Fenwick Island, right near the ocean, a perfect place for a weekend break.

We left Washington Friday afternoon. I drove and Megan told me where to go. And Ruby sat in the back seat, eating cookies, excited by the thought of spending a few days outside the city. Megan had told me very clearly that there were three bedrooms in her uncle's house—one for each of us.

It rained Saturday—a cold shower that blew in from the ocean. Megan and I sat and watched it out of the window, sitting close together on the couch.

"Where's our client?" I asked.

"Ruby? Watching TV. What are you thinking?" she asked quietly.

Everything and nothing. Thirty-two days earlier I had been married to another woman, living in a different apartment, and doing different work. I didn't even know the woman whose head was now on my shoulder. How could life change so much in a month?

"I'm thinking about my new life," I said.

And we both smiled.

Talk about it

1 **Work in groups of four. Each of you will be one of the people described below.**

It is six months after the end of the story. Since then:

- Michael has divorced Claire, who is now married to another lawyer called William, a man she has known for many years.
- Michael has spent a lot of time with Megan. He is going to ask her to marry him very soon.
- Mordecai Green has had a heart attack. He is fine now, but he can't work hard, so Michael is running the 14th Street Law Center with Mordecai as his assistant.
- Drake & Sweeney lawyers have done a lot of *pro bono* work with the homeless, and Michael is the main contact in arranging this work.
- A city television station is making a program about the *pro bono* work that the lawyers are doing in the city.

Student A: You are the TV interviewer. You will ask the three lawyers questions. You have these questions for Michael:
• What happened to make you leave Drake & Sweeney and work for the homeless?
• Did this change your home life at all? What did your wife and parents think about it?
Prepare more questions for Michael and the other two lawyers.

Student B: You are Michael. Prepare answers for the questions that the interviewer may ask about your life and your work.

Student C: You are Mordecai Green. Prepare answers for questions about Michael's work at the Law Center and the RiverOaks case.

Student D: You are Arthur Jacobs. Prepare answers to questions about Michael's work for Drake & Sweeney and how he was going to be a partner.

2 **Act out the TV interview.**

72

It is now one month after the TV program. Michael and Megan have got married. You are a reporter for a Washington paper. Write a piece about the wedding. Include background information about the couple, who they are, how they met, and the work they do.

Lawyer with a Heart Marries Head of Women's Center

It was a very happy day for hundreds of the city's poor and homeless on Saturday, October 6, when Michael Brock of the 14th Street Law Center married Megan O'Keefe from Naomi's Women's Center.

....

....

....

....

....

....

....

....

....

....

....

....

1 There are always homeless people, in rich and poor countries. Why is this? Work with other students and make notes on all the reasons you can think of. Use the pictures to help you.

Notes

2 Wars and natural disasters are, of course, responsible for many people becoming homeless. But even when there are no wars and natural disasters, there are people without homes. Imagine that you and your family are homeless. What problems would you have? Work with other students and add to the notes.

3 Think about your own country. Discuss these opinions with your class. Do you agree? Why (not)?

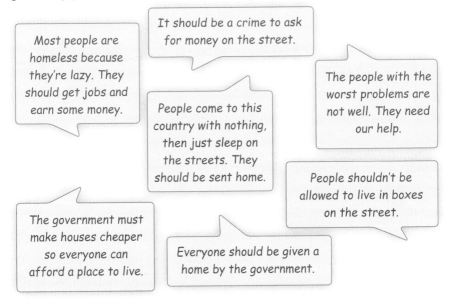

Project *Homeless*

4 What do you think should be done about the problem of homelessness in your country? Write a letter to your local newspaper and give your opinions. Use the headings below to help you.

Give your reason for writing

I am writing to ...

Explain the problem in your country

There are thousands of homeless people in our country.

What do you think should be done about the problem?

We cannot let homelessness continue. We need to take action to solve the problem.